Praise for *Behind the Hedges of Montecito*

"These glimpses into Montecito's past are entertaining and informative. The book is a charming reconstruction of the way things were, presenting the fruits of considerable research in a very appealing way. Let's hope it is just the beginning in a series, as there are many more Montecito stories waiting for Mrs. Griscom's graceful pen."

—Nevill Cramer
author of *Montecito Boy: An Irreverent Memoir*

"A longtime resident of the Santa Barbara area, Elane has researched the history of the estates and the lives of some who have made Montecito unique. Their individual stories make fascinating reading."

—Arthur N. Strahler
Professor Emeritus, Columbia University, New York

"This is a delightful, a fascinating book. Ms. Griscom discusses twenty or more Montecito estates, their settings, their histories, their owners past and present, their family lives together—all in a charming manner. The writing throughout is clear, compressed, and always graceful. All in all, *Behind the Hedges of Montecito* is an enviable work. Read and enjoy!"

—Donald Pearce
Emeritus Professor of English, UCSB

Behind the
Hedges of
Montecito

by Elane Griscom

FITHIAN PRESS, SANTA BARBARA, CALIFORNIA, 2000

Published by Fithian Press
A division of Daniel and Daniel, Publishers, Inc.
Post Office Box 1525
Santa Barbara, CA 93102

Cover photo of the guest house on the Wilkie estate, courtesy of Adèle Wilkie Collection.

LIBRARY OF CONGRESS CATALOGING-IN-PUBLICATION DATA
Griscom, Elane.
    Behind the hedges of Montecito / by Elane Griscom.
      p.   cm.
    ISBN 1-56474-317-9 (alk. paper)
    1. Montecito (Calif.)—Social life and customs Anecdotes. 2. Montecito (Calif.)
Biography Anecdotes. 3. Celebrities—California—Montecito Biography Anecdotes.
5. Montecito (Calif.)—buildings, structures, etc. Anecdotes.   I. Title
F869.M695G75   2000
979.4'91—dc21   99-30736
                                                      CIP

Acknowledgements

I would like to express my gratitude to all the knowledgeable people who have provided me with historical facts and guidelines.

These include David F. Myrick, author of *Montecito and Santa Barbara, The Days of the Great Estates*; Maria Churchill of the Montecito History Committee; Michael Redmon of Santa Barbara Historical Society; and David Griggs of Carpinteria Valley Museum of History.

ℰ Contents

Introduction 9

The Glen Oaks Story 13

At the Crest of the World 19

Remembering Amy du Pont 29

The Legendary Balladeer 33

Val Verde—A Golden Era Survivor 39

Montecito's Grande Dame 49

Stokowski's Secret Hideaway 57

In Pursuit of a Dream 67

A Tale of Two Artists 75

Resurrection in the Cemetery 83

ℰ INTRODUCTION

I NCLUDED IN this small volume are stories of some of the magnificent estates established in Montecito from the turn of the century to the 1930s. Accompanying the history of these mansions are personal vignettes of Montecito's colorful inhabitants, both past and present.

Most of the early arrivals were families of eastern and midwestern industrialists who were seeking refuge from winter weather, and the homes they created were at first considered only seasonal residences. Because of the mild climate and natural beauty, most of the newcomers eventually stayed on year-round, and Montecito was firmly established as the most desirable address in the Santa Barbara area.

Early in the century a large number of Mediterranean and Spanish colonial mansions were built, surrounded by luxuriant gardens reminiscent of Italy and Spain. The combination of climate and unlimited economic resources also brought world-renowned landscape architects such as Peter Riedel, Ralph T. Stephens, Lockwood de Forest, and the noted Italian botanist Dr. Francesco Franceschi.

In 1893 Dr. Franceschi formed the Southern California Acclimatizing Association in Montecito, equipped with greenhouses and experimental gardens that imported and grew a vast variety of semitropical plants and trees. According to Dr. Franceschi, this area is "the place where the largest number of plants from widely different climates have congregated to live happily together…and they combine to make display of vegetation that has no rival anywhere."

From the turn of the century to the present, Montecito has attracted people of great wealth and remarkable talent. For this reason we include a glimpse into the lives and contributions of some of the celebrated people who have made this their home over the years.

BEHIND THE
HEDGES OF MONTECITO

ॐ The Glen Oaks Story

GLEN OAKS is now a tranquil Montecito residential retreat shielded from East Valley Road by a barricade of rare trees and foliage. A far cry from 1868, when it was forty acres of open farmland bisected by picturesque San Ysidro Creek.

In April of 1868 Santa Barbara city officials deeded the entire forty acres to a former local tax collector named Miguel F. Burke for forty-nine dollars. An astute businessman, Burke sold the property three days later to one Elijah Stanton for $200. The open farmland known first as Field Place was bought and sold several times before 1884, when it was acquired by Samuel W. Gilcrest, who farmed the land until 1895. That year Dr. Alexander Blair Thaw and his wife, Florence Dow Thaw, of New York, purchased the property. Dr. Thaw was one of a family of eleven children who were heirs to a vast fortune from Pittsburgh coal and the Pennsylvania Railroad, where he held an executive position.

Thaw chose the prime, oak-covered acreage with its picturesque creek and splendid mountain views as the site for an elaborate twenty-one-room home for his wife and three daughters, a home that would allow sufficient room for their very active social life.

The name of the architect who designed Thaw's Glen Oaks home is cloaked in mystery, but evidence points to the internationally known Stanford White. White was the architect famed for the creation of

Collection of Pauline Richards

The original Glen Oaks mansion with its shingle-style exterior,
an innovation said to have been favored by
Stanford White on the East Coast.

New York City's original Madison Square Garden and Washington Arch, and five years earlier he had drawn up the plans for Dr. Thaw's summer home in Sparkhill, New York. Although the plan for Glen Oaks was not found in White's files, this was not unusual, as the architect frequently drew up plans for friends, such as Dr. Thaw, without keeping them in his official office file.

The shingle-style architecture of the Thaw house repeated the same design on the outer walls that Stanford White had used for Thaw's residential project on the East Coast. White often applied layers of shingles on exterior walls of his houses to create a textured appearance, exactly like that of the Glen Oaks house.

The family led an active social life in Montecito, and their estate was the setting for many important turn-of-the-century society events. Dr. Thaw was never involved in California medicine during the ten years of his residence here; however, he was very much involved in civic affairs and was on the board of directors of the *Morning Press* and other local businesses. Mrs. Thaw occupied herself with parties and elegant fancy-dress balls, which were always reported in detail in the society columns of the local press.

The idyllic Montecito lifestyle of the Thaws was shattered in June of 1906, when Thaw's erratic younger brother, playboy Harry K. Thaw, shot and killed Stanford White in the rooftop theater of New York City's old Madison Square Garden. The murder precipitated sensational stories in the press at home and abroad, and later even inspired a movie, *The Girl in the Red Velvet Swing*.

Harry K. Thaw had married the beautiful actress and showgirl Evelyn Nesbit in 1905. Evelyn had been a close personal friend of Stanford White for several years, and he had helped further her career. (She was known as the "girl in the red velvet swing" because she used the swing on stage in some of her performances.) Even though the relationship with White ended with her marriage, Thaw was consumed with jealously, and at a musical comedy performance where White sat conspicuously alone at a table, he walked quietly over to the architect and, in front of a stunned crowd, shot him three times.

Harry K. Thaw was found not guilty because of insanity and was committed to a New York State asylum. He and Evelyn were divorced, and for several years he was confined to an institution. After his release he continued to lead the life of an international playboy until his death in Florida in 1947.

In 1907, the year following his brother's notorious crime, Dr. Thaw sold his Glen Oaks home to James H. Moore, financier and president of the Rock Island Railroad. The Moores were familiar with the estate because they had leased it during the winter of 1905. After they purchased the estate, Lora and James Moore changed the name from Field Place to Glen Oaks. Ten years later James Hobart Moore died. However, his widow remained at Glen Oaks for a time and eventually married Harry F. Knight, a longtime friend of the family.

In 1924 William Hall (of the Prentice-Hall publishing company) purchased the property from Lora Knight and renamed it Hall House. Hall had several cottages built on the grounds in the 1920s, including a recreation house and a garden house. Through the years these cottag-

*Foyer of the Glen Oaks house. Beyond the Palladian arch is
the spacious landing with a grand piano.*

es have been enlarged, renovated, and made into charming homes
occupied by present-day Glen Oaks residents.

In the 1940s the Halls sold most of their property to developers,
retaining only the main house, a cottage used as a schoolroom for
their two daughters, and 3.6 surrounding acres. They kept a part-
time residence at Glen Oaks until 1952, when the house was sold
again, this time to wealthy cattle ranchers named McKinley who had
five other homes and seldom spent time in Montecito. By 1952 most
of the estate's original acreage had been subdivided into one-acre
lots on which new homes were built.

Among the surviving early structures is the carriage house used to house Dr. Thaw's horses and carriages, which still retains much of the original exterior design.

In 1956 the Glen Oaks house was sold to Pauline and Maurice Richards. The Richardses expanded the kitchen to incorporate a comfortable dining area for their family of nine children, and also added a laundry room. Pauline Richards, who appreciated the functional and beautiful design of the home, said, "I love the floor plan because every room is light and airy with a flow of space that makes it ideal for entertaining."

The basic design of the house was an open, rambling plan with a dramatic foyer enhanced by a Palladian arch. This symmetrical arch pattern was repeated throughout the home in doorways, alcoves, and even in windows on the west side framing the garden and pool views.

The raised landing in the foyer, visible through the Palladian arch, was large enough to hold a grand piano. "When we entertained with formal parties, this spacious landing area would accommodate a five-piece orchestra," recalled Pauline Richards. To the left of the foyer was the ballroom-size living room and, on the right, a dining room that could easily accommodate three dozen guests at dinner.

With her children grown and in homes of their own, Pauline Richards decided, somewhat reluctantly, to sell the house and move to a condominium. Still, she misses Glen Oaks and reminisces about the wonderful years spent there. The house recently has been completely remodeled by the new owner.

During the Hall family's occupancy, one of the famed Moody sisters, Harriett, an architectural designer, was commissioned to renovate and expand the cottage that had originally been built by Lora Moore Knight for use as a Christian Science reading room.

The cozy Schoolhouse Cottage is now the home of architect Gary Banks and his wife, Kathy. The Bankses have completely redesigned the landscape of their surrounding acre. Kathy notes that due to their many trips to Ireland over the years, their home has now taken on the ambiance of an Irish cottage, while still retaining the charm and warmth of a typical classic California bungalow.

"I love the serenity of Glen Oaks," says Kathy. "The homes are not

Collection of Pauline Richards

Pauline Richards arriving in style at a Glen Oaks
costume ball in the 1970s.

pretentious; the trees and natural beauty of the surroundings are what's important. There's a sense of nature here that gives me a feeling of continuity."

Shaded by oak, pine, cedar, and sycamore trees, Glen Oaks property owners enjoy strolling thorough their quiet, woodsy neighborhood along a road that narrows to one lane as it bridges a creek. It meanders past a variety of landscape designs, from natural ground cover studded by rocks and oaks to meticulously tended lawns with colorful flower gardens. Glen Oaks, though just a few minutes from town, remains an oasis, a peaceful retreat for its fortunate residents.

ℰ At the Crest of the World

ONE MISTY spring day in 1928, a small single-engine plane circled the foothills of Montecito west of Ladera Lane. On an earlier visit the pilot had surveyed this same property on foot while looking for a future landing site. His choice for an improvised strip was the grassy field he now approached—well below the main house on a gentle slope cleared of brush and trees. Flying low, he brought the trim silver plane in on a final glide with the nose high and left wing low, giving him a better view of the ground. Bouncing uphill over the rough terrain, he rolled at last to a stop.

Charles A. Lindbergh, otherwise known as the "Lone Eagle," had come to Montecito to pay a second visit to a friend and financial benefactor, Lora Moore Knight, who owned not only the field and the mansion on top of the hill but all the surrounding acres.

Born in Illinois in 1864, Lora grew up in Chicago, where her wealthy father, Edward A. Small, was a corporate lawyer. Together with his law partner, James Hobart Moore, he held controlling interests in an impressive list of "blue chip" firms of the day, including National Biscuit, Continental Can, Diamond Match, Union Pacific, and Rock Island Railroad, among others.

A romance had blossomed between the tall, attractive Lora and her father's partner, James H. Moore, and when she was eighteen years old she and Moore were married. In her honor Moore named

View of Cima del Mundo with a field below later
converted to a landing strip.

his elegant summer home on the shores of Lake Geneva, Wisconsin, Loramoore. Around the turn of the century, the Moores decided to escape the harsh Wisconsin winters by purchasing a winter haven of their own in California. They decided on an estate in Montecito named Field Place, which they had rented previously. Soon they changed its name to Glen Oaks because of the woodsy beauty of the setting.

Moore, who was considerably older than Lora, died at their summer home in July of 1916, leaving Lora a ten-million-dollar inheritance from his estate. By this time she preferred living year round in California, so she sold Loramoore soon after his death.

In January of 1922 a long family friendship culminated in a second marriage for Lora Moore with a wealthy St. Louis widower,

Collection of Martha Clyde

Harry Hall Knight and Lora Moore Knight, financial backers who helped make Lindbergh's historic transatlantic flight possible.

Collection of Martha Clyde

Harry H. Knight. The wedding took place in the elaborately decorated garden of the Glen Oaks house. However, because of Knight's business interests, they made their home in St. Louis (where in 1925 Lora created a stir when she commissioned the construction of a fifty-two-room castle).

Besides operating his own successful brokerage firm, Harry Knight was an aviation enthusiast who took flying lessons and was president of the St. Louis Flying Club.

Early in 1926 Knight was approached by a young pilot known as "Slim" Lindbergh. The tall, lanky, and determined Lindbergh, then flying air mail between Chicago and St. Louis, dreamed of being the first to fly across the Atlantic but desperately needed financial backing to make his transatlantic flight a reality. He had heard of the influential Mr. Knight and knew of his passionate interest in aviation.

In the hope of obtaining funding, he called on Knight at his brokerage office to ask for financial help. Harry Knight, impressed with Lindbergh, found the proposed transatlantic flight an exciting idea. Knight was enthused enough to immediately place a call to his banker friend, Harold Bixby, who also had an interest in flying. Lindbergh's project, flying an airplane from St. Louis to New York to Paris, excited Bixby also. Knight was able to persuade Lora and Harold Bixby, among others, to provide enough financing for Lindbergh to have the *Spirit of St. Louis* built to his specification, thus enabling him to make the historic transatlantic flight.

Unfortunately, the brief Lora Moore-Harry Knight marriage ended in a Reno divorce in 1927, just before she moved into her hilltop home, Cima del Mundo (Crest of the World), off of Montecito's Ladera Lane.

Lora Knight's grandniece, Mrs. James De Loreto of Santa Barbara, recalls that "Aunt Lo was always cheerful and had a sense of humor. We visited Cima del Mundo frequently, and I have vivid memories of parties and card games in a Japanese teahouse that opened to lovely vistas of ocean and mountains." Mrs. Knight had purchased the teahouse in Japan on one of her round-the-world voyages and had it dismantled and shipped to Cima del Mundo.

"We would have picnics on top of the covered reservoir too,

because of the splendid view," said Mrs. De Loreto, "and for these picnics, Aunt Lo's chauffeur would bring up white linen and silver service." (The teahouse and a greenhouse with a rare collection of cymbidiums were later destroyed in the 1964 Coyote Fire.)

Lora Knight had purchased the Ladera Lane acreage in 1917, but it wasn't until 1924, after she sold Glen Oaks, that construction began on the house she named Cima del Mundo. The house was so named because of its location on the crest of a hill with uninterrupted views of ocean, islands, mountains, and the city of Santa Barbara.

To make certain she was building in exactly the right spot, she is said to have spent many nights camping out on the property. When at last she selected what she considered to be the perfect site to take advantage of the views, she commissioned Pasadena architect Myron Hunt, whose specialty was the design of hacienda-type houses, to create a tile-roofed Mediterranean-style residence with three wings enclosing a courtyard.

Of all the Montecito survivors of the twenties, Cima del Mundo is one of the very few that has not been noticeably altered. It remains basically as Lora Knight's architect designed it in 1924. A walk-in safe on the lower level still contains the original blueprints of the house. They show a total of eleven bedrooms: four in the main house, five in the servants' quarters, and an additional two-with-bath in the lower level laundry rooms for servants.

This was the age of Prohibition and, on the plans, a small room off of the living room is labeled a "trunk room." The gregarious Mrs. Knight loved parties, and the trunk room is thought to have actually concealed a built-in bar.

Century-old oak trees enhance the front of the house and its circular drive. The foyer and den are richly paneled in oak, and a galleria leads to the spacious, beam-ceilinged living room with windows designed to capture the sunset. The manor house bedrooms have marble fireplaces, original light fixtures and, a relic from the elegant past, a callbox to summon servants.

Adjoining Lora Knight's master suite was a sitting room where, in summer, windows could be lowered and recessed into the wall, transforming the area into an outdoor sun porch. The floor and walls of the bathrooms gleamed with white tile, circa 1925. A built-in scale was permanently set into the floor of Mrs. Knight's suite.

Wrought iron on the windows was a later addition, put there for safety rather than decoration. Lora Knight, who had remained a good friend of the Lindberghs, feared for her own safety after the tragedy of the Lindbergh baby's kidnapping. Not only did she cover the windows with wrought-iron bars, but entries to crawl spaces in the foundation were also closed off with wrought iron. Unique for the 1920s was her electric-eye system, which protected the exterior grounds of the property at night. The entrance to the estate from East Valley Road was guarded by a gatekeeper who lived in a picturesque stone house that can still be seen just inside the original entry gate.

On the basement level she installed a game room with a bowling alley equipped with a miniature set of pins for children of visiting relatives. Lora always enjoyed and encouraged the visits of her young nieces and nephews because she loved children; the tragedy of her life was the loss of her only son, Nathaniel Moore, who died in a traffic accident while in his mid-twenties.

Lora Moore Knight was described as a charming and extremely generous woman, albeit possessed of a somewhat restless spirit that prompted her to change her residence frequently. In 1928, a year after building Cima del Mundo, she began construction of yet another home on Lake Tahoe's Emerald Bay. The design of the Lake Tahoe house, which she named Vikingsholm, was influenced by her travels through Scandinavian countries. Vikingsholm is now part of Emerald Bay State Park.

Lora Knight continued to spend winters in Santa Barbara, summers at her Lake Tahoe estate, and autumn months in a home she built in Reno. It was surmised that the practical Mrs. Knight had established a Reno residence not only for tax advantage, but to facilitate her divorce from Mr. Knight. In 1944, a year before her death, she sold Cima del Mundo along with all of its furnishings to her longtime neighbors Ernest and Louise Fleming Duque, of the Portland Cement Company.

In 1963 Avery Brundage, of Olympic Games Committee fame, was interested in purchasing the property. But Father Von der Ahe, a Jesuit (and a member of the Von's supermarket family), had been nurturing the concept of a college for the training of Catholic priests on this magnificent wooded site, and Mr. Brundage withdrew his bid. Fulfilling Father Von der Ahe's dream, the property eventually became the 138-acre College of Reina de la Paz (Queen of Peace) Jesuit Novitiate.

The new educational complex took shape in 1965 on a hill above Lora Knight's former manor house. It contained an administration building, chapel, dining hall, dormitory, maintenance buildings, and a forty-two-by-seventy-six-foot swimming pool.

The former Lora Moore Knight residence was maintained in its original pristine condition by members of the Jesuit Novitiate, who through the years used it for retreats, recreation, and conferences. However, the property was eventually sold because of a drop in student enrollment and the changing needs of contemporary religious training.

Thirty-eight acres on the northeast section of the property went to Casa de Maria for a religious retreat house; the rest is to be subdivided for residential estates.

In the meantime, Lora Knight's house, Cima del Mundo, remains much the same as when she last walked through the door, perched serenely on its hilltop awaiting whatever changes the future may hold.

Charles A. Lindbergh was a frequent visitor to the Santa Barbara and Montecito area in the years following his historic flight. He had first landed at Earl Ovington's airport (where the Santa Barbara Municipal Golf Course is now) and had Ovington drive him to Lora Knight's Montecito house so he could check out Cima del Mundo for a good landing site. The guest book of John J. Mitchell, Jr., husband of Lolita Armour and a member of a prominent Chicago banking family, recorded several visits by Lindbergh. Mitchell had been a director of United Airlines for many years and had a strong interest in aviation. Lindbergh was also a guest at Wright S. Ludington's Val Verde estate on Sycamore Canyon Road, arriving in July and staying until after Fiesta.

During his visit with Lora Knight, Lindbergh enjoyed taking her family members and staff for short sightseeing flights in his plane. Lora let the others go, but she refused to accompany them. When he left Cima del Mundo, he bade them all a memorable goodbye by doing a

Carpinteria Valley Museum of History

Lindbergh at Carpinteria airport with mechanic Wes Hearn, inspecting Ryan Aircraft replica of Spirit of St. Louis, *1928.*

complete loop over the field. This event was recorded in a home movie now in the archives of the Smithsonian; the Santa Barbara Historical Society also has a copy of this film.

In April of 1928, after leaving Lora Knight's estate, Lindbergh stopped to refuel in Carpinteria, as it was a fifty-two-minute flight from there to Los Angeles. In the 1920s, Carpinteria had its own airport on a bluff at the east end of town. The mechanics at the Carpinteria facility worshipped him—and when word got out that he was at the local airport, most of the town gathered at the field to welcome him. One of the original hangars still remains on Carpinteria Avenue and is now in use as an auto repair shop.

Santa Barbara Historical Society

Lindy in 1928.

ℰ Remembering Amy du Pont

PEGGY McMANUS Houghtaling has driven the same car for fifty-eight years. It isn't the only car she has ever owned, but it is by far the best and certainly the most enduring.

In 1941, Peggy was a twenty-year-old singer and aspiring actress who also happened to be a protégé of Amy du Pont, heiress to the Delaware du Pont fortune. When Peggy saw the car in all its glittering splendor in a magazine advertisement in 1940, the wealthy and generous Miss du Pont promptly ordered the coral-colored Buick from a dealer in Hollywood.

"It arrived in Santa Barbara by train in 1941. Amy and I went down to the depot, waited for it to be unloaded, and then we drove up State Street—I'll always remember that day. I visited Amy shortly before she died in 1962, and she got such a kick out of seeing that Buick convertible again."

Amy du Pont, the last surviving member of the Delaware du Pont dynasty, came to Santa Barbara in 1922. A horse enthusiast, she was drawn to Montecito because of the beautiful riding trails that wound through the rugged foothills. She also set up a riding school in Hope Ranch and continued riding until one day she was thrown from a horse and severely injured.

Miss du Pont and the musical McManuses became close friends because of their common love of music. Peggy Houghtaling's father was a successful composer, and her mother a singer. Miss du Pont took over Peggy's schooling when she was a small child, sending her to the best of private schools and, in later years, financed her so that she could try for a career in Hollywood.

"As a child, I used to stay at Amy du Pont's house when my family was off on a musical tour, and it was fun," Peggy recalls. "She had a wonderful sense of humor. We shared a love of animals, and she gave me two horses and a number of white Sealyham dogs that she had raised."

Miss du Pont shunned publicity and preferred to entertain small groups of close friends. "We had lunch every Sunday with Amy—she was a very informal person and just wanted to be called Amy," says Peggy. "She was also completely without vanity. Instead of going to a hairdresser, she had the maid cut her hair—and she hated to shop for clothes. She had chosen the maid carefully; the woman was exactly the same size, so Amy could send her into town to buy her clothes. As a result, she sometimes looked a little funny." When Peggy was married in 1942, Amy du Pont invited five hundred people to the lush gardens of Casa del Sueño for the wedding ceremony.

Peggy McManus Houghtaling, who lost her beautiful daughter, Winks, in a tragic accident a few years ago, still lives in Montecito and still drives her 1941 Buick convertible, accompanied by her fifteen-year-old dog, Baby, and her memories.

Casa del Sueño, Amy du Pont's "House of Dreams," was originally designed in 1917 for Reginald Rives of New York, who commissioned a nationally known architect, Reginald Johnson, to draw up the plans. Johnson was the architect who designed the Santa Barbara Biltmore Hotel in 1925 and the J.P. Jefferson house (now the Music Academy of the West). Johnson's original plans for the house show broad stucco walls with occasional symmetrically placed balconies, windows, and terraces—all reminiscent of the Mediterranean influence in California.

Miss du Pont bought Casa del Sueño in 1930 and lived there until her death in 1962. A gifted horticulturist, she made extensive landscaping improvements and hired as many as fourteen gardeners to plant lawns bordered by spectacular shrubs and flower gardens. Ruth St. Denis once entertained by the reflecting pool in a special concert. Amy du Pont's love of cacti inspired her to nurture a vast assortment of

Collection of Peggy Houghtaling

*The bride is Peggy McManus Houghtaling, escorted by her father,
Joseph McManus. The wedding was held in the gardens of
Amy du Pont's Montecito estate in 1942.*

rare plants, and in 1930 she commissioned a well-known local artist,
Mrs. Christian Herter, wife of a former secretary of state, to paint a
mural on the dining room walls, patterned after her cactus garden.

These were the days when elegant estates of Montecito frequently
opened their gates for tours to benefit local charities. Amy du Pont was
especially known for her generosity and supported many cultural
organizations as well. In the 1970s her former estate, Casa del Sueño,
became the home of Dorothy and Burl Ives, who had moved to
Montecito from Los Angeles.

ℰ The Legendary Balladeer

B URL AND DOROTHY Ives moved to Montecito in 1974 and occupied Amy du Pont's Casa del Sueño. Mrs. Ives described their home as a charming and comfortable place with none of the cold and formal ambience sometimes built into the houses of grand estates.

During their years in Montecito, the Iveses traveled thousands of miles doing benefits and concert tours abroad and at home.

One memorable evening in September of 1985, as the house lights dimmed at the Lobero, America's greatest balladeer appeared on stage in a one-man show, *The Mystic Trumpeter—Whitman at Seventy*, based on the life and works of poet Walt Whitman. "When Burl's make-up was finished, it was as if Whitman was standing before the audience— a complete transference—as if the balladeer had become the poet," said Mrs. Ives.

Dorothy and Burl Ives decided to write the script of *The Mystic Trumpeter* themselves because they couldn't find a playwright who knew the poet and his work as intimately as they did.

"I doubt that there's anyone in the country who knows Whitman the way Dorothy does," Burl said. "The scripts we received from play-wrights didn't capture Whitman. So finally, in desperation, we did it ourselves."

No stranger to the stage, the white-bearded Ives (who, in his prime, stood six feet tall and weighed 300 pounds) had starred in

Collection of Dorothy Ives

Burl Ives in his role as Walt Whitman.

thirteen plays on Broadway, including the stage version of *Cat on a Hot Tin Roof*. He won an Academy Award for his supporting role in an epic western of 1958, *The Big Country*.

Their Montecito home, Casa del Sueño, was completely hidden from East Valley Road by trees and hedges. The main house was situated to take advantage of splendid views of the Santa Ynez Mountains to

*Casa del Sueño with the reflecting pool where Ruth St. Denis
once gave a dance recital.*

the north and the Pacific to the south, and was surrounded by five
acres of mature gardens designed by its former owner, Amy du Pont.

It was not unusual for the blond and vivacious Mrs. Ives, an animal
lover, to greet visitors in the midst of the commotion made by two
large German shepherds and four smaller (and more gregarious) dogs.

Beautiful panels of stained glass framed the carved front entry door,
patterned after the murals in the dining room inspired by Miss du
Pont's cactus garden. Formerly an interior decorator in Beverly Hills,
Dorothy Ives pointed out that "all the colors in the house were related
to these murals; in all, there were nine different shades of blue."

She explained that she and Burl had done some remodeling on
Casa del Sueño. "What I tried to do was to keep it pretty much within
its original structural beauty because it was designed by the noted
architect Reginald Johnson. I felt the love and warmth of the house
when I first stepped in the door. Most of our changes were just opening

up small areas—like the kitchen. I did add a deck upstairs, a downstairs terrace, and some small windows were transformed into French doors."

The library was probably the most "lived-in" room in the house, with its large fireplace, comfortable fireside chairs, and roll-top desk. Shelves of books lined the paneled walls, making it a warm and cozy room for Burl Ives to indulge in reading, one of his favorite pastimes.

Heidi, one of the German shepherds, opened the front door, came in, and settled down in the study near Burl, who was relaxed in his favorite armchair by the fireplace. "Heidi learned to turn the knob and open the door by herself," Mrs. Ives laughed.

Burl Ives's rich voice remained as melodious in conversation as it was in song, and his sense of humor was sharp. Although he was suffering intense pain from arthritis, his spirits were still upbeat. Every so often in concert, he said, he would forget the words to a song, but it didn't worry him "because in my songs I'm telling a story, not just memorizing words—other words will fit in."

Dorothy commented, "We're not home as much as we'd like to be, but we love this house. It's a very homey place. Burl and I are very simple people; we don't like to dress for dinner—we just like to be comfortable when we're at home because we always have to be dressed when we're on the road."

Burl added, "We once had a butler who came in formal dress— Dorothy was in a robe and I was sitting here watching TV. He wanted to serve our dinner in the formal dining room," Ives chuckled. Can you imagine me in my long underwear with a butler serving me? We didn't hire him as a butler, but he had a butler complex and wanted to butt. The wonderful thing about Montecito is that people can be themselves if they allow themselves to be. It's the nice thing about this place— nobody bugs you; they let you do your own thing. It's marvelous," he said enthusiastically.

The legendary Ives was the quintessential American entertainer whose life story as adventurer, musician, balladeer, and Oscar-winning dramatic actor parallels the plot of a Horatio Alger novel. Ives, with his warm and kindly manner, leaned back in his chair and patiently answered questions he had probably answered a thousand times before.

About his roots he said, "I was born on a farm, and then we moved into this little Illinois town, Hunt City Township." He related how he began to sing as a small child, gathering with his parents and six brothers and sisters around the old family pump organ to sing hymns. "He heard the hymns while still in his mother's womb," Dorothy added. "From early childhood he could carry a tune, sing on pitch, and was in demand at church and social affairs. There wasn't a conscious decision to go into music; it was instinct."

Ives was thinking about writing a sequel to his 1945 book, *The Wayfaring Stranger.* "I thought of doing my own critique of the book. It would be fun because I certainly know myself better—I have a better understanding of why I wrote this or did that. I know now.... But writing is a very tough job because it is time-consuming, and you really have to get everything else out of your mind and get away from everybody. That book brought me up to the time I went into show business, and my life since then has been quite different.

"Starting as an amateur on radio back in Indiana, I always used the 'Wayfaring Stranger' tag, and it was a nice theme song for the show. It sort of gave you the idea that a fellow came along and sang songs and then left—a nice idea for a fifteen-minute radio show of ballads. But I don't sing 'Wayfaring Stranger' much anymore. It doesn't make much sense within the context of a concert to sing that song.

"I'm not a gifted composer," he added, "but I'm a good editor. If the wrong words and wrong kind of phrase are in the context of a song, I can feel it. I started writing ballads years ago. When I was a kid I knew so many of the old classics that when I compared my own work to those songs, I said, 'Well, I can't write.' I stopped because I knew that what I was doing wasn't up to what I had within me."

The late Burl Ives is now a legend whom poet Carl Sandburg once called the greatest folk ballad singer of them all, and whose life story reads like one of his own ballads. From childhood on he pursued something that he was "good at" and, as a wayfaring minstrel, he was led by his musical talent down the path to enduring fame and fortune.

❦ Val Verde—A Golden Era Survivor

D R. WARREN AUSTIN in earlier years was aptly described by a biographer as "tall and good looking, with a voice not unlike that of Cary Grant and that same debonair quality—a non-venal Svengali with dark eyes and hair, and a cleft in his chin."

Now, at age eighty-eight, the doctor remains personable and charming, his idealism undiminished, despite the frustration of a long and costly struggle to donate his historic Montecito property, Val Verde, to Santa Barbara County.

Val Verde is a survivor, one of the few intact estates remaining from the golden Gatsby days when Montecito was an enclave reserved solely for the rich and famous, a life-style that has all but vanished. At a time when the natural beauty of this area faces the prospect of becoming another paved-over, subdivided Los Angeles lookalike, Dr. Austin is determined to preserve Val Verde's house and spectacular gardens for the use of generations to come. The doctor visualizes the house and its surrounding 17.5 acres open to the general public with a limited number of visitors per year.

Born in Seattle in 1911, Dr. Austin grew up in Cosmopolis, a small lumber town on the Washington coast, where his father worked as a civil engineer. A brilliant scholar, he was able to enter the University of Washington at age sixteen to study architecture, but his interest later switched to journalism, enabling him to work his way through the

Elane Griscom

Dr. Austin at Val Verde with his classic Rolls Royce.

University of Washington as a reporter for the *Seattle Post-Intelligencer*. After completing a bachelor of science degree, he moved on to the University of Michigan Medical School.

He recalls with whimsical humor why he settled on a medical career. "It was during the Depression, and medicine was the longest course of study I could find. I liked attending school and, under the circumstances, wanted to remain as long as possible." He interned at Kings County Hospital in Brooklyn, New York, became an internist and endocrinologist, and did postgraduate studies in Europe. "In my day you weren't considered a finished doctor unless you took postgraduate courses in Vienna," he adds.

Immediately after the bombs fell on Pearl Harbor, Dr. Austin enlisted in the Army and was assigned to what sounded like a chilly post—the North Atlantic Division of U.S. Engineers. He found to his surprise that everything north of the equator was classified North Atlantic; in 1942 Lieutenant Austin was ordered to the Bahamas as head medical officer at the Nassau Army Hospital, which had been set up in a converted hotel.

The two years Dr. Austin spent in the Bahamas coincided with the

Duke of Windsor's term as governor. (HRH Edward VIII, who abdicated the British throne in 1936, was assigned to the Bahamas in 1940 after four years of self-imposed exile in France.) Dr. Austin recalls, "I first met the duke through his aide-de-camp, Major Gray Phillips, who broke his little finger in a freak bicycle accident and came to my hospital for treatment. We became good friends, and he invited me to all sorts of dinners and parties and eventually introduced me to the Windsors, who were charming hosts. I found the duke to be easygoing, and I liked him very much. It was quite a change for me, a country boy, to be dining with the duke." The duke had trouble with the American pronunciation of "lieutenant," so following Austin's jocular suggestion, the duke promptly promoted him to captain.

Until Dr. Austin arrived and became their personal physician, there had been no local doctor in the Bahamas, so the duke and duchess were flown to the United States when they needed medical attention. As an endocrinologist well ahead of his time, Dr. Austin was asked to prescribe hormones for the duchess.

"Most of the duke's problems were aches and pains from frequent falls off of his polo pony," he recalls. He also helped the duke overcome a slight speech defect by recording his speeches and playing them back until they eliminated the stammer. In return the duke taught him to tie the fashionable Windsor knot in his neckties—"They are folded twice over, which makes a bigger knot," Dr. Austin explains.

He remembers the duchess as being a strong presence, not beautiful in the Hollywood fashion, but a gracious hostess with a sense of humor. She was reserved, however, and no casual acquaintance presumed to call her Wallis.

Dr. Austin and the duchess were always partners at bridge. "I played so poorly, I think she wanted to protect the other guests from me, and they played for high stakes that I couldn't afford.

"I was frustrated during those two years because I thought I had enlisted to help the war effort, and here I was attending black-tie dinners every night." After two years in the Bahamas, however, Dr. Austin was reassigned to Europe, where he served as surgeon with General George Patton's Third Army from Omaha Beach through the Battle of the Bulge to Czechoslovakia.

While planning ahead for a location to set up his postwar medical practice, Dr. Austin had narrowed his choices to either Seattle or Santa Barbara and had sent for information from both chambers of commerce. The inviting film he received, plus the gentle climate, helped him decide on Santa Barbara.

Earlier, at a Nassau farewell party in Government House given for Dr. Austin by the Duke and Duchess of Windsor, he mentioned his decision to eventually establish a medical practice in Santa Barbara. The duke said, "You must get in touch with my dear friend Beryl Markham, who is living in Montecito. She has recently married and is now Mrs. Beryl Shumacher." Beryl had spent some time with friends in Nassau in 1941 and was a close friend of Gray Phillips, the duke's aide-de-camp. Because of Beryl's sensational transatlantic solo flight in 1936 and her many unconventional romances, she had already received more than her share of worldwide notoriety.

When Dr. Austin arrived in Montecito late in 1945, he checked into the Montecito Inn and phoned the Shumachers, who invited him to dinner that same night. Learning of his connection with the Duke of Windsor, Beryl insisted that he move out of the inn and stay with them. At that time the impecunious Beryl and her husband, Hollywood writer Raoul Shumacher, were house-sitting at the Monastery, Leopold Stokowski's part-time home in Toro Canyon. Dr. Austin recalls life in the rustic retreat with the volatile Shumachers and describes Beryl as a vibrant personality. "She had grown up in Africa enjoying the freedom of a native and was not concerned with conventional moral standards; she liked going about the house without clothes." He recounts how the charismatic Beryl Markham, a tall and beautiful blond, wove an irresistible romantic spell on all of the men who met her. "When she came into a room, the other women present became invisible. Naturally, women didn't like her very much."

For the next few months he stayed on with the Shumachers while setting up his first medical practice in an office on Chapala Street. Eventually he rented a house for himself, and in 1948 opened offices in the new Montecito Medical Center, becoming the community's first medical doctor. "I was single then and made house calls morning, noon, and night with scarcely any sleep." He was active in his medical practice until the late 1970s, when he "tapered off slowly and recruit-ed another doctor to take over."

He recalls the beginning of his romance with Heath "Bunny" Hor-ton, the beautiful heiress to the Chicago Bridge and Iron Company fortune. Like the scenario for a Hollywood film, they met in the 1950s on a westbound train in Utah. Both were en route to a Valentine's Day party in Sun Valley, Idaho, hosted by the wife of the popular orchestra leader Eddie Duchin.

At the time, Dr. Austin was living in the redecorated gardener's cot-tage on the grounds of Val Verde, which he had rented from the owner, art collector and philanthropist Wright Ludington. "Ludington was a hy-pochondriac who relished having a doctor close at hand," he comments.

Dr. Austin and Bunny Horton were about to be married in 1956, just at the time that Wright Ludington decided to sell Val Verde to Marjorie Buell, a horsewoman from Denver. She realized too late that it wasn't the right place to keep her horses. Without even moving in, Buell sold Val Verde to Dr. Austin and Bunny Horton. The Austins had one daughter, Dorothy, who presently lives in Washington State.

Dr. Austin jokingly refers to Val Verde's Mediterranean architectural style as "Texaco Spanish." The villa was originally commissioned by a wealthy coffee trader from New York, Henry Dater, and completed in the early 1900s. The two-story, tile-roofed house, somewhat reminiscent of a classic Tuscan villa, was designed in 1892 by architect Bertram Goodhue, who later created the Los Angeles Central Library.

Dater had originally hired Pasadena landscape designer Charles Gibbs Adams to create the garden. The landscaping was substantially altered in 1925, when the second owner, Charles H. Ludington (who bought the property for less than $100,000) brought in his own land-scape artist, nationally known Lockwood de Forest, to redo the grounds. Ludington also changed the estate name to Val Verde (Green Valley) from Días Felices (Happy Days), which he thought sounded too much like the name of a saloon. After Charles Ludington's death in 1927 the estate was inherited by his son, Wright Ludington.

The gardens of Val Verde are a horticultural wonderland care-fully planned by de Forest to integrate with the house and frame the mountain views. There are imported as well as indigenous plants

Lockwood de Forest's reflecting pool, classic columns visible on the terrace.

and trees—a wealth of live oak, sycamore, Moreton Bay fig, Monterey cypress, royal palm, and olive trees. Where the land slopes to Cold Springs Creek, indigenous wild nasturtiums and lilies of the Nile add a splash of color.

In the July 1998 issue of the magazine *House Beautiful*, Val Verde is described as "Lockwood de Forest's masterpiece." It is also included as one of eight carefully selected gardens in the book *American Landscapes of the Country Place Era* by landscape historian Robin Karson. The author considers Val Verde one of the most important California estates remaining from the pre-World War II era.

The house and gardens are the result of collaboration between De Forest and Wright Ludington, who agreed to change the front approach to the house in order to allow space for a circular, walled motor court. An arch bordering the court frames glimpses of a fountain overhung with native California live oak trees, some of the many that proliferate on the grounds, their beauty enhanced by careful pruning. On the mountainside below the living room terrace is a large rectangular

Elane Griscom

One of Val Verde's prized oak trees.

pool with the bottom painted black to create mirror-like reflections.

A unique exterior feature that connects house and gardens is the row of twelve-foot-tall square columns that extend from both sides of the main veranda. They look as though they are remains of old ruins that might at one time have supported statuary. However, Dr. Austin explains that their sole purpose has always been to create constantly changing patterns of light and shadow.

On the south side of the house, landscaped divider strips separate the swimming pool from parallel rectangular reflecting pools, giving the illusion of floating gardens. When the Austins first purchased the estate it consisted of nine acres, and they expanded the grounds to seventeen, for aesthetic reasons as well as for privacy, by purchasing land that bordered on Rivenrock on the east.

Seated in his living room, where soft light from a Moorish-tiled atrium filters through French doors, Dr. Austin reminisces about the highlights of his life and the celebrities that have graced it from time to time. An avid art collector, Dr. Austin has filled this warm and inviting room with an eclectic assortment of priceless antiques and artifacts, and there are numerous mementos of his wife, with whom he shared Val Verde until her death in 1991.

Photos of a glamorous young "Bunny" Austin are displayed on the concert grand piano along with autographed photos of their good friend Dame Judith Anderson, whom he first met backstage in New York when she appeared in *Mourning Becomes Electra*. A theater seat inscribed with Judith Anderson's name, a souvenir of a Lobero Theatre fund-raising auction, stands near the piano and is a reminder of the many years he was involved with the Alhecama and Lobero theaters as a producer and actor.

As a young doctor interning in New York, Austin became a passionate play-goer, spending much of his off-duty time at the theater. After he settled in Santa Barbara and established his medical practice, his love of the theater did not diminish. He was one of the original founders of the Alhecama Theater, lending a hand as a backstage prop man and even loaning furniture and artifacts from his home as props. His acting career was launched as an understudy for the lead role in the production of *The Time of the Cuckoo*. When the star left the production shortly before opening night, Austin made his stage debut in the lead role. This began a long acting career at the Alhecama and, later, at the Lobero.

Through the years the Austins generously contributed to many local cultural organizations such as the Alhecama Theater, the Lobero Theatre, the Music Academy of the West, and the Santa Barbara Symphony. Dr. Austin frequently opened the gardens of Val Verde for the benefit of local nonprofit groups. The estate has also hosted celebrities and occasionally provided an elegant backdrop for movies and television. A television mystery starring Olivia de Havilland, "The Screaming Woman," was filmed on the grounds a few years ago. A long list of past celebrities who have attended Val Verde social events includes David Niven, Janet Gaynor, and film actress Margaret Sullivan, among others.

Polish concert singer Madame Ganna Walska, of Lotusland fame, was a longtime neighbor as well as patient of Dr. Austin, and a somewhat demanding friend. Dr. Austin recalls that she called him to the Biltmore Hotel late one night to an "emergency" that turned out to be the treatment of a hangnail on her friend, chanteuse "Hildegarde," who was entertaining at the hotel. "Ganna took my prescribed hormones and, like most of my patients, she lived to be a hundred years old," he says. "I believe she thought of me as her aide-de-camp as well as her physician and called on me frequently in the years before my marriage to escort her to local parties and theatrical events."

Dr. Austin keeps his medical license operative in California as well as in Washington and Michigan, where he also spends time. He summers from May until the first of September on Canoe Island in the San Juans and, sometimes in early spring, visits a home he still owns in England. Winter months he prefers to spend in Santa Barbara at Val Verde.

An ardent conservationist, Dr. Austin owns fifty-acre Canoe Island in Washington State's San Juan Islands, dedicated to the preservation of open spaces and native trees, plants, and animals. Thirty years ago on this island he established a young people's summer camp that teaches French history, language, and customs, enabling the campers to make comparisons with their own culture. Dr. Austin recently placed the island and camp in a perpetual trust in the state of Washington, a generous gift gratefully accepted and appreciated by foresighted local, state, and national officials.

At the time of this writing the Santa Barbara County Board of Supervisors, heeding only the behest of a small but vocal opposition group, has seen fit to deny Val Verde the protection it needs to be preserved as a historic landmark. This bureaucratic decision was made despite the favorable Val Verde report from Caltrans; despite the favorable environmental report; despite the approval of the County Planning Commission and the support of numerous historians, horticulturists, architects, university professors and concerned citizens who spoke in favor of Val Verde.

The loss of Val Verde will mark the end of an era when wealthy and far-sighted citizens dedicated themselves to preserving the community's cultural treasures. In this case, however, *noblesse* refuses to *oblige*; undaunted, Dr. Austin plans to persevere. As the first resident medical doctor to set up practice in Montecito, he has been a valued physician to many. He has remained a good friend and active supporter of the cultural well-being of the community. Warren Austin's dream is still to see the splendor of Val Verde preserved and made available for the benefit of generations to come.

𝒞 Montecito's Grande Dame

T HE LATE Dame Judith Anderson became enchanted with the Santa Barbara area in 1929 while appearing at the Lobero Theatre in Eugene O'Neill's *Strange Interlude*, but it wasn't until 1946 that she moved here. "I've always loved this place," she said. "I'm not from movies. My life has been the stage, and I wanted to get away from Los Angeles, where I had been making films."

Dame Judith Anderson, one of the greatest actresses of the century, whose portrayal of Medea made theatrical history, was the first Australian-born actress ever to be given the Most Excellent Order of the British Empire. The ceremony, which she described as "the greatest event of my life," took place at Buckingham Palace in July of 1960, when she was given the insignia of Dame Commander by Queen Elizabeth II.

Excelling throughout her career in classical roles, she played Lady Macbeth opposite Sir Laurence Olivier and also appeared with Sir John Gielgud in *Hamlet*. In 1948 she was awarded a Tony on Broadway for Best Actress in the title role of *Medea*, a modern adaptation written by her favorite poet, Robinson Jeffers. The fury and passion of her performance thrilled audiences and made *Medea* one of the great moments of theatrical history.

Although Dame Judith was well past her ninetieth birthday at the time of this interview, her complexion appeared remarkably fresh and as smooth as the proverbial English rose. Still, the petite and fragile

Montecito History Committee

*Dame Judith Anderson as Gertrude in a
scene from* Hamlet.

actress apologized for her appearance. "I haven't make-up on. I'm terribly slow and lazy today," she said as she led the way into the bright and cheerful room where she now spent most of her time. Moving gracefully, she settled into a comfortable sofa with her pet dachshund, Bozo, curled up beside her. "I can't live without a pet. I've had animals all my life," she commented, giving him an affectionate pat. This, her last home, was a gabled English cottage on San Ysidro Lane known as Lone Oak, a house hidden from the street by shrubbery and surrounded by an acre of overgrown, out-of-control garden.

Warmed by the morning sun, the white walls of the room reflected

Montecito History Committee

Dame Judith's last home on San Ysidro Lane in Montecito.

the traditional blue of her treasured delft collection. "When I added this room to the house I wanted to put in a fireplace, but all the models I looked at were quite modern and much too large. Finally the salesman said, 'Here's this small blue thing I can show you.'" Dame Judith pointed to an exquisite free-standing fireplace decorated with delft blue tiles. "That's the blue thing, and it's finished in pure delft," she said delightedly.

On a corner table were family photos of nieces and nephews, an illustration of her father's family estate in Scotland, and a watercolor of her childhood home in Australia. Despite her warmth, quick smile, and witty repartee, a thread of melancholy ran through the conversation as she spoke of friends and family who had died.

"My father was born in Scotland, and my mother's family were English. They migrated to Australia because of the milder weather conditions, so I was born in Adelaide. It was a mile square then; now it's all high-rise and changed. My immediate family are all gone, and I'm the only one left except for a gaggle of nieces and nephews.

"As a child in Australia, I wouldn't go to school—I was a terrible child; showing off all the time," she recalled, a mischievous glint in her eyes. "I wasn't pulled in any direction—I just had this burning desire to perform from the time that I first came out of my mother's womb. She didn't want me; I was the youngest of four, and she didn't want any more children. But from the beginning I loved to recite and I loved to sing. My mother's family were all very musical," she said, her voice making every utterance sound like a line of Shakespearean dialogue. Dame Judith, during her early years in Australia, won gold and diamond medals in drama competitions. In 1918 her mother, "who had a passion for theater," took her to New York. There they lived in a rooming house, and her mother found work as a seamstress, leaving Judith free to pursue her acting career.

"I came to this country with energy and ambition but no money. I haven't been back to Australia since my last brother died," she said sadly. "I just don't like to think about it. My friends are all gone. It's awful; I have no family left in Australia except for nieces and nephews. Dear friends that I grew up with in Australia are gone—my friends in New York are all gone, and I'm on my way out."

Dame Judith was twice married and divorced. Her first husband was Benjamin Lehman, a University of California professor. They married in 1937 and were divorced in 1939. In 1946 she married Luther Greene, a theatrical producer and Carpinteria rancher. During their marriage she bought a ranch in Carpinteria and built a "pink palace on a hilltop." "I could see the ocean, mountains, everything from up there through its massive windows," she reminisced. "Below the house the land was green with lemon and avocado groves, and the fiery sunsets were magnificent. But the marriage ended in divorce and other things went wrong, so I sold the place. But I still miss that ocean view."

Comparing work in films with the theater she said, "In the theater you read your play and fall in love with it.... You go to rehearsal every day and you are a family together with the rest of the cast. Your audience is part of your heart and soul, and they tell you when you are wrong, which is wonderful; they support you and you feel you've completed something. In the theater you can use the entire stage and you are unlimited with space, voice, gesture, and movement.

"In films you are restricted, and there's a trick to it that I have not learned. I still don't know how to manipulate for films. I remember working years ago with Barbara Stanwyck and Walter Huston. In this picture I was in love with her father and she didn't like me. When we were introduced she raised one eyebrow. When Stanwyck saw the rushes she said, 'Where's my first scene?' She felt that her raised eyebrow told the whole story of the relationship—but I wouldn't want to play a scene like that."

Reflecting on movies she had been in, she said the part she most enjoyed was that of the malicious housekeeper, Mrs. Danvers, in *Rebecca*. "At the time I was very new in the film industry. It was a wonderful picture produced by David Selznick and had Hitchcock, a great director, with a marvelous cast that included Sir Laurence Olivier."

About her performance in the Academy Award-nominated picture *King's Row*, starring Ronald Reagan, she smiled and said, "In movies, unless you have a scene together, you don't necessarily meet the other artists and there isn't time for socializing. Afterward I never saw the picture.

"I wish I had a beautiful face," she reflected, "but my nose is too large and my eyes are too small. An unattractive woman has to work doubly hard. Still, people tell me I have a mobile, interesting face that will never grow monotonous."

When subjects arose that she didn't want to address she made her point by putting her finger to her lips to indicate silence. She sealed her lips when the soap opera "Santa Barbara" was mentioned, making it very clear that she didn't want to discuss her work in the well-known series, where she portrayed society dowager Minx Lockridge.

Although she was best known for her portrayal of evil characters and reportedly had an explosive temper off-stage, she was also a compassionate member of the local community. She put her energy into raising funds for local theater, especially for the Lobero, where she established the Dame Judith Anderson Fund, designed to bring serious theater to Santa Barbara.

Besides the 1929 version of *Strange Interlude* at the Lobero she also starred there in *Mourning Becomes Electra* in 1932 and *Medea* in 1948. In 1970 she premiered her portrayal of *Hamlet* at the Lobero before taking it to New York's Carnegie Hall. "I like the emotional roles because they permit the unleashing of one's feelings," she commented. She also did benefits for the Ensemble Theater, where she encouraged and inspired its young performers.

She described her three-bedroom English cottage near the San Ysidro Ranch as a very comfortable house in which to live. "A wealthy lady, well known in Montecito, built this place for her lover in 1929," she said. "It was named Lone Oak because of the beautiful old oak tree in the garden. For years I had it well taken care of. The branches were tied with thick wire to hold it together, but it finally blew down; it was very old."

The house, completely hidden behind the shrubbery and woodsy growth, reflected the solitude she had come to enjoy. She was once quoted as saying that she would rather be at home with books and music than go to the most fashionable party in town. Life in the Santa Barbara area suited her very well. She had the solitude she cherished, yet, when she so desired, she could participate in theatrical activities such as the filming of television's "Lifestyles of the Rich and Famous," and the popular soap "Santa Barbara."

"When I moved into this house in 1964 it had a beautiful garden, and gardening was my joy. Now it's overgrown with weeds," she said, gazing mournfully through the window at the withered remains of the flower garden. "I can't get a decent gardener; they come late and leave early and always have their hands out. I fell on the stairs here at home and fractured my back. Since then I haven't been able to work in the garden, and it is an absolute heartbreak for me to see it in ruins." Still, from the weed-choked garden there were beautiful mountain views. In addition, she had planted mimosa, native to Australia, around a circle of stones where the lone oak had once stood.

A lovely early portrait of Dame Judith brightened the hallway opening into the formal living room. This room was large and high-ceilinged, with thick adobe-like walls that seemed like a dramatic stage set. Furnished with objects d'art and antiques, the living room had space for her grand piano in one corner and a loft stocked with books above the far end of the room.

"You'll find dead flowers all over the place—because they die so beautifully," she said. "They don't hold their perfume, they don't hold their color, but they keep their form." The ethereal dead flowers, arranged in a vase on the living room mantel, looked like puffs of smoke. "They come from a sunny corner of the yard where there is a rare and unusual shrub and, when the blossoms come out, they are bright red, feathery, and delicate," she explained. "These flowers on the mantel have been there for years. They die beautifully; you see, they are immortal. People don't die like that." In her rich voice she quoted appropriately from the nineteenth-century English poet Walter Savage Landor: "…I warmed both hands before the fire of life. It sinks and I am ready to depart."

Dame Judith Anderson died at home in January of 1992, but memories of her unique talent, like the rare blossoms she treasured, will linger on indefinitely.

ℰ Stokowski's Secret Hideaway

ENVELOPED IN an aura of romance, a half-century-old house high in the rugged foothills of Montecito's Toro Canyon was the secret hideaway of world-renowned symphony conductor, Leopold Stokowski. The modest cottage was his private Shangri-La, and it was here that he shared a passionate affair with film star Greta Garbo and later romanced British pilot/authoress Beryl Markham.

With a touch of irony the maestro christened his cottage the Monastery. It was a retreat from the pressures of his career, where he could find relaxation not only in romantic interludes, but also in gardening and carpentry.

Tall, slender, and with a radiant smile, the charismatic but moody Stokowski charmed ladies of all ages throughout his life. Born in London in 1882, the son of an Irish mother and a Polish father, Stokowski studied violin and piano in his early childhood and by age ten was playing Bach on the organ. He attended London's Royal College of Music and continued his studies in Europe. His professional career began at age eighteen when he was appointed organist for Saint James's Church in London.

In 1905 he came to New York to be organist and choirmaster at Saint Bartholomew's Church, and it was in New York that he met and married his first wife, noted pianist Olga Samaroff. (Born in Texas, Olga had been christened Lucy Hickenlooper.) Three years later he signed a contract with the Cincinnati Symphony. In 1912 he moved on to become conductor of the more prestigious Philadelphia Symphony, a position he held until 1936. His appearance as a conductor was described as theatrical and spectacular. He broke a baton by accident during a concert before the 1929 season and realized how much freer he was when he expressed himself solely with his hands. From then on he conducted without a baton.

In later years, as a free-lance conductor, Stokowski presided at innumerable concerts around the country and made thousands of recordings. Always interested in new technology, he made some of the very first experimental stereo orchestral recordings.

In 1937 he appeared in the film *100 Men and a Girl* starring Deanna Durbin. This first venture into Hollywood led to a meeting with Walt Disney, who contracted him to appear in the 1940 production *Fantasia*, a film featuring concerts of classical masterpieces. This fulfilled a dream of Stokowski's—to bring classical music to the masses.

Stokowski first visited Santa Barbara in the 1930s when he came to work with Montecito musicologist/composer Henry Eichheim. The maestro became so enchanted with the area that in 1933 he decided to buy an eleven-acre parcel of land in Toro Canyon for $10,000. According to Santa Barbara County records, he invested another $10,000 in 1934 and purchased an adjoining seven-acre parcel from Santa Barbara builder Robert M. Hyde.

Construction of the house began in 1935, when builder Robert Hyde completed the living room, kitchen, and bath. Because the 1930s were the height of the Depression, Hyde was able to find an abundance of low-cost unskilled labor for the project.

Stokowski himself loved doing hands-on work and became quite an expert at gardening, mixing mortar, and laying bricks, and he eventually took over planning the entire construction. The basic U shape of the house was patterned after an earlier design Stokowski had done for his Beverly Hills home, and he continued to make modifications for years.

From its vantage point in the foothills of the Santa Ynez mountains the house was sited to take advantage of dazzling views of the Pacific Ocean and Channel Islands, as well as Toro Canyon and a

Elane Griscom

Painting of Leopold Stokowski's Toro Canyon cottage.

glimpse of the Santa Barbara harbor. Situated on a sloping hillside, the living room and kitchen areas were on a lower level of the hill, and a five-bedroom wing was planned above on higher ground in order to share the ocean views.

Stokowski also put in a swimming pool and patio between the protective wings of the house. Electric heaters and fireplaces took the place of central heating. All the mature trees surrounding the house were planted by the maestro himself to frame magnificent views, including some very old olive trees that he moved from a lower level and replanted on either side of the front lawn.

At the time Stokowski built the house, his first marriage (in 1911) to pianist Olga Samaroff (aka Lucy Hickenlooper) had ended in divorce. In 1926 he married his second wife, Evangeline Johnson of the Johnson and Johnson pharmaceutical family.

Before starting construction on the Monastery, Stokowski and Evangeline had stayed at Ronald Colman's Montecito guest ranch, and it was thought at the time that Stokowski's charming one-story, board-and-batten house might have been inspired by Colman's original San Ysidro Ranch cottages.

When the house was completed Evangeline and Stokowski moved in with their two little girls, Sadja and Lyuba. While living there, the Stokowski children amused themselves with horseback riding, painting, and sculpting. They even managed to preserve their tiny footprints in the new, wet patio cement.

Throughout his lifetime, Stokowski attracted many women, and his romances made headlines. His love affair with Greta Garbo began in 1937 and precipitated his divorce from Evangeline. The secluded Toro Canyon ranch house became their private weekend retreat.

Longtime Santa Barbarans remember seeing Garbo and Stokowski together at a performance at the Lobero Theatre. Afterward they walked down Anacapa Street to dine at the El Paseo restaurant. (Garbo's outfit was described as "unique:" she wore knickers and a felt hat with a wide brim.)

Eventually this much-publicized affair with Garbo came to an end because, as Stokowski explained, "She was too melancholy." However, they remained friends until, at age sixty-three, the famed musician married "poor little rich girl" twenty-one-year-old Gloria Vanderbilt. After the marriage Garbo came to see him in Beverly Hills and asked if she could rent the Monastery, but he refused because Beryl Markham was ensconced there at the time.

It was thought that Gloria Vanderbilt lived at the ranch with Stokowski after Beryl moved out, as so many of her personally autographed books still remained. Vanderbilt and Stokowski also spent time at Villa Calafia, an elegant Mediterranean-style estate located near Toro Canyon on Foothill Road. Despite his new bride's insistence that he sell the ranch because it held too many reminders of past romances, he couldn't bring himself to part with it. "There is too much of myself in it," he reportedly told a friend.

In April of 1945, Beryl Markham, of *West with the Night* fame, moved in as a rent-free caretaker/tenant with her partner in a troubled marriage, Raoul Shumacher. This was an arrangement made through a mutual acquaintance of Shumacher and Stokowski. Beryl Markham loved the place and, according to the Mary Lovell biography *Straight*

Elane Griscom

*A night on the town. Stokowski leaving the Lobero with
Garbo en route to El Paseo for dinner. For this
occasion she was said to have worn knickers
and a floppy-brim hat. Circa 1939.*

on *Till Morning*, Markham said, "It's the loveliest house in the world."
According to the book, she loved the ranch more than any place she
had ever lived because the setting reminded her of her home in Africa.

From the mid-1940s until it was sold in 1953, the property was pri-
marily in the hands of caretakers because Stokowski's illustrious career

Stokowski at the Lobero with Martha Graham and
Lotte Lehmann, circa 1940.

kept him abroad much of the time. However, the Toro Canyon ranch was never out of his thoughts, and he constantly sent detailed instructions to caretaker Robert Lopez for maintenance and for the planting of rare trees that he frequently shipped from exotic places he visited.

Stokowski was said to have visited there frequently in 1946 during the Shumachers' occupancy, adding to the rumors about the brief love affair between the maestro and Garbo-look-alike Beryl Markham. Markham was also said to have enjoyed the freedom of doing her household chores in the nude.

Finally, in November of 1953, Stokowski sold the house to a friend for $32,000, including the art deco furnishings. He left behind a number of interesting books and many unreleased phonograph recordings from his symphonic career.

The collection of books included a volume of poetry by Pulitzer

Prize winner Zoe Aikins, the only woman among four screenwriters on Garbo's 1937 film *Camille*. The inscription reads: "For lovely Garbo in appreciation and remembrance of Marguerite Gautier; Zoe Aikins, Christmas 1938." Apparently Garbo had spent Christmas at the ranch just after finishing her role as Camille. There were also Yogananda philosophical books inscribed to both Garbo and Stokowski. Books from a later period were signed "Gloria Stokowski, 1946"—the year after she and the maestro were married.

Among memorabilia Stokowski included with the house were two rare pieces from his collection of far-eastern musical instruments. On the patio wall was a gamelan gong from Indonesia. A huge Japanese Buddhist resting bell in the dining room was loaned for use as a set decoration in the original version of the classic film *Lost Horizon* starring Ronald Colman.

When he moved out of the ranch house, Stokowski donated some of his musical instrument collection to the Santa Barbara Museum of Art's Eichheim Collection, now part of the special collections of the music department of the University of California, Santa Barbara, along with many of his unreleased recordings.

Several years ago the ranch was visited by one of Stokowski's daughters, Sadja Stokowski Greenwood, then a San Francisco physician. She was fascinated because the place remained almost the same and brought back a rush of early-childhood memories. The room that was once her mother's still contained Evangeline's art deco desk. It is easy to visualize Beryl Markham seated there at her typewriter, struggling over a manuscript in the late 1940s.

Sadja found that her father's bedroom remained as he had left it except that the room no longer held his Steinway. The bookshelves he had installed and his sketches of a table designed for the room were still there.

The bedroom window design was also unusual; when opened, they slid down into a wall panel and completely disappeared from view, giving the feeling of being outdoors. A fragrant blossoming jasmine vine he planted still framed the window of the master bathroom. For much of the year he could leave the windows down and feel that he was sleeping outside. Facing east, it was a good sunrise-viewing room and, in summer, a fig tree, also planted by Stokowski, provided shade just outside the door.

The bathrooms, with their low-slung plumbing (a design Stokowski felt was more natural), had also remained unchanged, Sadja found. The built-in dressing table that Garbo and Beryl Markham had used was still in place. It is easy to fathom why Markham loved the ranch house with the nostalgic "world without walls" atmosphere she had enjoyed in Africa.

The inner patio featured a huge, unique "organ fireplace" designed by Stokowski in the shape of a pipe organ, with bricks set in a vertical pattern to give the impression of organ pipes. The organ fireplace burned like a campfire; Stokowski reportedly said he planned it that way. "You can see sparks going up and reflecting on the bricks; it makes a marvelous outdoor fireplace." The pool terrace was high enough to have a view over the roof of the living room to the ocean and islands beyond.

At the time Stokowski sold the house, there was a storage basement containing some of his belongings, including recordings and 1930s furniture. In the cozy library on the west side of the house was his Persian fireplace, so called because of its Islamic arch. This room took advantage of a lovely distant view of the Santa Barbara harbor, and in winter it was warmed by the afternoon sun. The library connected directly with the kitchen through a "secret door" invisible from the kitchen.

Stokowski's French windows with avocado-colored paint had remained, as well as the open-beam ceilings and walls and the adjoining terrace outside used for dining *al fresco*. When Stokowski re-visited the house in the 1950s, bringing his two sons by Gloria Vanderbilt, Stanislaus and Christopher, he related how Greta Garbo had done some of the brickwork. While watching Stokowski, Garbo had said, "It doesn't look hard; let me try it," and ended up building a section of the garden wall.

The brick-and-mortar fireplace in the living room is shaped like the acoustical backdrop of the Hollywood Bowl. A photo was used in a PBS television documentary about former tenant Beryl Markham, fully clothed, sitting contentedly in front of this fireplace. Stokowski loved curved lines and used them often in his designs. The living room floor was laid in a curved pattern of bricks and reflected the patina of wear through the years.

Generous with his musical talent, the London-born conductor was named director of the Pacific Coast Music Festival in Santa Barbara in 1955 and received a special award from the city for the four memorable concerts he directed in the sunken gardens of the Santa Barbara courthouse. He dreamed of holding an annual music festival here that would rival Tanglewood and become as renowned as Salzburg. However, the dream failed to materialize because of lack of financial support.

After the divorce from Gloria Vanderbilt, Stokowski remained single, and his personal life became a very private affair. "I never talk about that side," he once said to a friend. "The achievements of great artists always became the property of the public, but their private lives belong to themselves."

When Stokowski died in 1977 at the age of ninety-five, he had been supervising construction of a new home high above the French Riviera, in a setting reminiscent of Toro Canyon, where he had enjoyed the pristine privacy of a personal Shangri-la.

ℰ In Pursuit of a Dream

THE WILKIE ESTATE, in an exclusive Montecito enclave off of East Valley Road, has been the backdrop for innumerable grand events, but none more unique than the pageant planned for the dedication of the "Wedding-à-la-Carte" chapel in October of 1998. A garden party reminiscent of the Gatsby era was attended by 300 guests dressed in wedding-white who gathered to celebrate the chapel's inauguration.

Every detail of the chapel's design and its presentation sprang from Adele Wilkie's creative imagination. "I wanted an event that would dramatize and document life's great happenings. I especially wanted to depict a spiritual path from birth to death," she explains.

Early in his marriage to Adele, Leighton Wilkie, aware of his wife's creative talents, encouraged her to always pursue her dreams. Following his philosophy through the years, she continued to create elegant surroundings and memorable events. Her latest dream was transformed into the crystal-and-white miniature chapel on wheels, which she whimsically named "Wedding-à-la-Carte."

Her inspiration for the mini-chapel first came about because people searching for a romantic spot for weddings constantly called her for advice. "Santa Barbara has always been a favorite location for weddings, and young people obviously need to have a proper and affordable setting for an outdoor wedding.

Elane Griscom

*A scene from the elaborate pageant planned for the
"Wedding-à-la-Carte" dedication, a marriage
ceremony enacted in the mobile chapel.*

"It happens that my granddaughter's husband is in the asphalt-blacktop business and, when he came to resurface my driveway, I was reminded that he had lots of mobile equipment kept in storage near their home. I visualized using one of these mobile units for the construction of a portable chapel, and I also hoped that my granddaughter, a former executive at Northrup Corporation, would help coordinate the mechanical aspects," she relates. "I felt it would be a chance for her to use her business ability and still be at home with her children."

The result of Adele's design is a delicate gazebo-like structure with gothic-shaped aluminum columns supporting a curved canvas top. The shape, she explains, was inspired by the roof of the Sydney, Australia opera house. "I've designed it so it can be used with different backdrops, including a stained-glass window. It is completely wired for lighting with a crystal chandelier suspended over the altar making it suitable for a variety of occasions from weddings to memorials." With its own 18-by-16-foot hydraulic, self-leveling trailer, it can be moved to any location.

Adele's husband, the late Leighton Wilkie, was a brilliant inventor and manufacturer who began inventing tools for the automotive repair market while still in his teens. Mr. Wilkie founded the Do All Group with headquarters in Des Plaines, Illinois, developing it into more than seventy industrial supply stores worldwide. A metal-cutting bandsaw he invented in 1933 remains one of the most widely used tools in industry today. "His avocation was anthropology relating to man's use of tools throughout history," Mrs. Wilkie reflects. "He held the theory that man evolved through the use of tools, and the quality of life improved as the use of tools expanded, and his theory is illustrated in a permanent exhibit in Chicago's Museum of Science and Industry." Leighton Wilkie carried his interest in anthropology still further by initiating underwriting for studies conducted by Dr. Louis Leaky, Jane Goodall, and Dian Fossey, among others whose works were eventually funded by the National Geographic Society.

Like many families of midwestern and eastern industrialists lured by the mild California climate, the Wilkies came to Montecito to establish a winter home. They purchased a twelve-acre Montecito estate, La Sorpresa (The Surprise), named by the original owner, Edward S. Patterson, in 1912. The purchase price included an oil painting built into the wall above the living room fireplace, and the Wilkies won out over a rival bidder by offering to buy the painting as well. Today the property consists of three beautifully landscaped acres surrounding the main house, and a short distance away is La Folie (a country place for fun and frolic), probably the most magnificent guest house in all of Montecito.

After the Wilkies decided in the 1950s to sell their Illinois home and make the Montecito estate their permanent residence, Leighton Wilkie had a small guest house built on the property in order to experiment with the use of solar energy for heating.

"The solar-heated guest house was an advanced idea, years ahead of its time. It wasn't very successful though," Mrs. Wilkie adds. "At first this was just going to be a small house for the use of guests and visiting family members. But when my husband finished his solar experiment he gave me carte blanche to do whatever I wanted with it. It was a wonderful challenge," she recalls.

It was then that her imagination took off. She had first thought of just adding on a studio where she could work on her innumerable arts and crafts projects, including her clever miniature replicas of French court life. Inevitably her love of French history, art, and architecture prompted her to plan a much grander use for the house—a dream that evolved into a four-bedroom replica of a French palace.

Entering Adele Wilkie's little palace, La Folie, you are instantly transported into the glittering eighteenth-century world of Marie Antoinette. La Folie is a jewel-box reproduction of Le Petit Trianon, the little palace in the gardens of Versailles built by Louis XIV as a secret place to romance Madame Dubarry, among others, and later used as a refuge from court life by Marie Antoinette. "The creation of La Folie took considerable time and planning," recounts Mrs. Wilkie.

Working with Adele on the project was eighty-nine-year-old George Charney, an old family friend who also had moved to Montecito. Charney had been art editor of the Chicago News for thirty years and was a fine artist and designer with a scholarly knowledge of eighteenth-century French furnishings. "We were in total agreement on all the construction and design aspects; anything I could dream up George knew how to achieve," she comments. "We had an excellent builder who knew nothing about French design but was good at adapting space, and we had fine artisans like Bob Plude, who learned to marbleize, produce faux malachite (the green mineral used for artifacts), and taught us an improved method of gold leafing. My late nephew, Britton Wilkie, painted the murals, the harmonizing window shade paintings, and also decorated the doors. The entire house became an art form. We were all artists—creative people with great energy and imagination.

"After years of planning and waiting for building permits, construction of La Folie was finally completed in 1992. It was fortunate that I was able to have the original ceilings raised and the walls pushed out; it proved helpful later," she says. Her project more than doubled the size of the original building. Now over 4,000 square feet, the glamorous guest house has four bedrooms, five bathrooms, a library, foyer, drawing room, solarium, kitchen, maids' quarters, and a two-car garage.

Elane Griscom

*The resplendent dining room with
marble floors, crystal chandelier
and a floor-to-ceiling view of
the surrounding gardens.*

During the years Adele Wilkie traveled the world with her husband
on his business trips, she had acquired beautiful decorator accessories,
antiques, paintings, and other artifacts to import and sell wholesale
through a Chicago representative. She learned Italian well enough to
negotiate on her own for priceless, colorful crystal chandeliers, a reward-
ing endeavor that helped her acquire a personal collection that lends a
museum quality to the decor of La Folie.

Frequently visiting Mexico in their travels, the Wilkies had depos-
ited $10,000 in a savings account in Laredo. When it was time to
withdraw the money they found they could only receive devalued
pesos in exchange. The pesos were almost worthless unless they could
be spent in Mexico. With one million pesos and only one day to spend

Adele Wilkie seated beneath her portait
in the drawing room of La Folie.

them before they had to leave for home, Mrs. Wilkie frantically tried to think of something to buy.

Fortuitously she came across a marble distributor with a large supply of fine-quality, imported marble. She knew she could put it to good use in the guest house, so she decided to spend her pesos on marble. When the dealer asked how much she wanted shipped, she realized she had no idea of the amount she could use. Making a quick decision, she told the perplexed salesman to send "enough to fill two garages." It proved to be a brilliant guess. Enough marble arrived to cover several guest house floors. Because of the marble purchase, family members still refer to La Folie as the "Garage Mahal."

The house is now a graceful creation in a neoclassic French style with windows looking out on the beautifully landscaped lawns and gardens. The stunning entrance hall, with its white marble floors and gold swan-based table, brings you into an eighteenth-century pavilion where Marie Antoinette would feel perfectly at home. The entry opens into a drawing room that sparkles with lighthearted decor done in pastel colors edged with gilding and complimented by naturalistic paintings of figures and landscapes borrowed from the rococo era.

"I had to search for just the right table to be centered in the entry hall," Mrs. Wilkie says. "A future project I have in mind will be a book on Sèvres china to place on the entry table. Photos of each hand-painted Sèvres portrait plate will include a biography of the person pictured and will describe the position that each held in the court of Versailles. It will be a work of love and lots of fun to do."

All of Mrs. Wilkie's personal touches are inspired and unique. Soft blue, the dominant color in the front bedroom, is repeated in the rich fabric of bedspread, upholstery, draperies, and paintings done with a delicate touch.

A focal point in the room, framed in a shadow box, is one of the miniature built-to-scale scenes she delights in designing and assembling. The shadow box room, with minuscule furnishings in the style of Louis XVI, has on either side of the tiny fireplace two framed miniatures which, at first glance, appear to be portraits of Louis XVI and Marie Antoinette. On closer observation the faces are those of Adele and Leighton Wilkie, painted by her artist nephew, Britton Wilkie.

The Napoleon bedroom, decorated in vivid hues of green and blue, had a painting of Napoleon crowning himself emperor of Rome hanging over the empire-style antique bed. "The face on the man on horseback is actually that of George Charney, and the face in a bedside portrait of Marie Antoinette is mine—these were some of the fun things we did," Adele adds. All of the bedrooms have imported gold fixtures and elaborate built-in linen closets.

A modern exception is the gleaming white kitchen that opens to a delightful solarium—a perfect setting for entertaining. Furnished with one-of-a-kind white wrought-iron tables made by Italian artisans, each table is topped by a matching umbrella, another of Mrs. Wilkie's original designs. The umbrellas are illuminated with hundreds of tiny lights, as are trees and shrubs in the surrounding garden. At night the effect is a glamorous fantasy world enhanced by the garden fragrance of roses, jasmine, and gardenias.

*The solarium, showing in detail one of the
elaborate wrought-iron tables topped
by a matching umbrella, another
of Mrs. Wilkie's designs.*

Mrs. Wilkie combined her artistic ability, her knowledge of French history, and a tremendous amount of energy to make La Folie a bedazzling reincarnation of Le Petit Trianon. The result is truly a work of art and a lasting tribute to the combined talents who created it.

ℰ A Tale of Two Artists

THE LIVES of Montecito artists Hanne Brenken and Ricardo Wiesenberg have encompassed all the drama of an award-winning screenplay. Surviving war, prejudice, and political fallout, they somehow managed to find each other in mid-life on the Mediterranean island of Elba.

When they first visited Santa Barbara in 1985 they stayed at El Encanto Hotel and were captivated by scenery that reminded them of the Tuscany region of Italy, where they had once lived.

When they returned to this area ten years later they found that the former Bartlett Polo Clubhouse was for sale, and having a weakness for historic houses and a need for a large studio, they soon purchased it from the widow of famed Bauhaus artist Herbert Bayer.

The house belonged to an era when polo was the newest and most popular game in town. With polo fields proliferating on the Mesa and in Hope Ranch, Montecito fans wanted a field more accessible to them. In 1913 prominent sportsman William H. Bartlett optioned thirty-four acres along Middle Road and had architect Francis T. Underhill draw up plans for what was to be the Santa Barbara Polo Club.

The club opened for business at the end of 1916 with splendid views of the mountains and the Rincon from the playing field and viewing deck. It remained a clubhouse until 1932, when the Depression made its operation unfeasible and it was converted to a residence.

Courtesy of Hanne Brenken

The historic Bartlett Polo Clubhouse on Middle Road in Montecito.

The house today, with its white, solid concrete walls, appears little changed from its halcyon days as Montecito's first polo club.

Brenken and Wiesenberg, besides being internationally known artists, delighted in buying and renovating historic houses, and the former polo clubhouse is an example of what they both find important: an historic background in a beautiful setting.

The rooms are enhanced by their art, and the warm glow of afternoon sunlight filters in and illuminates Wiesenberg's classic landscapes and Brenken's haunting, surreal creations. Each represents a uniquely different philosophy and technique in his or her work. Wiesenberg's full-length portrait of Hanne hangs in the front entry hall, and it completely captures the essence of her persona.

Genial and gentle, Hanne is the daughter of a wealthy German industrialist. Born and raised in western Germany near Dusseldorf, she married at age eighteen and with two children suffered through the war years while her young husband, a pilot, was serving on the Russian front.

Hanne had always wanted to be an artist, but from the beginning her family disapproved. In her excellent English she explains, "My father did not think of painting as a serious occupation. As a result I couldn't express my creativity, and I was very unhappy during my early years. For an outlet I wrote and published my short stories and poems." Her first husband also objected to time spent on art studies and wanted her to remain at home full time with their two children.

As a result of years of family opposition Hanne was forced to become a completely self-taught artist. In 1958 she was able to hold a one-person show, which brought immediate acclaim from critics and collectors. In the early 1960s she became a well-known abstract "hard edge" painter, and by 1969 her work was on display at Munich's Museum of Modern Art along with pop artist Roy Lichtenstein. Her work was also exhibited solo and in group shows throughout West Germany.

Tall, vibrant, and silver-haired, Ricardo Wiesenberg, son of a Jewish father and young gentile woman (who had dreamed of becoming a dancer), was born in Germany in 1926, and he faced harsher circumstances than Hanne. Wiesenberg's father was unwilling to marry his girlfriend and fled to America. Left alone after having the baby, destitute and desperate, Wiesenberg's mother had a nervous breakdown. She was institutionalized, and her young son was placed in foster care. Wiesenberg never met his father, and later he learned that his mother had been a victim of Hitler's euthanasia program. His paternal grandparents finally located Ricardo in Berlin and took him to live with them in East Germany.

Ricardo had always wanted to become an artist, but at an early age he was encouraged by his godfather to become a photographer instead. Wiesenberg says, "That was when I learned that a good photograph is better than a bad realistic painting."

In 1944, when he became old enough to be drafted into the German army, the Nazis discovered his Jewish parentage and sent Ricardo instead to a labor camp in the Harz Mountains, a place for people who were half-Jewish, members of the resistance, or war criminals. They were put to work building a factory hidden deep inside the mountains. "We had to make artificial gasoline for the rockets," he recalls. "We worked inside an old iron mine, and it was a very hard time. We were allowed little sleep and almost nothing to eat."

When the camp commander saw the end of the war approaching,

he began releasing the inmates. Wiesenberg traveled by rail and on foot to Berlin, but found it under siege. He comments, "I felt like Dante in hell—some unseen force was taking me to these awful places, but somehow I managed to survive."

He traveled more than 200 kilometers to his grandparents' home in East Germany. When he reached their house he found that his grandfather had died and their home was occupied by Soviet pilots. "My German grandmother had lived in Poland, so she was able to speak the language fluently. Polish is close enough to Russian that she could communicate with the pilots, who adopted her as their *babushka* [grandmother]." After the war, when the Polish army pushed all German residents out of their homeland, the Russian pilots helped his grandmother escape. They put her on a train that would take her to a nursing home in the west. She eventually died there.

While in East Germany Ricardo managed to study at the art school in the town of Halle and later at the Academy of Fine Arts in Dresden. "As much as I loved my art studies, I couldn't accept the propaganda of the new communist regime. The trouble started when I didn't agree with their politics. East Germany declared me an enemy of the state, and in 1952 I escaped to West Germany."

Wiesenberg began his new life with no artistic credentials and no money, but because of his exceptional talent he was eventually accepted at the Academy of Fine Arts in Munich, and in 1958 he received the prestigious title of *Meisterschuler*, an honor given to the school's best student. "I studied in three different academies for over eight years, and I feel academic training has been a great help to me." Ricardo's work was exhibited every year between 1960 and 1978 at the Munich Museum as well as other galleries, and was added to the permanent exhibits of two German museums. During this time he also became expert at art restoration, working on landmarks for the German government and restoration of paintings for museums and private collections.

Fate intervened in the separate lives of Hanne and Ricardo in 1970, when each decided to visit a friend on the island of Elba. This led to their romantic first meeting on the island, and after a reunion in Munich they have been together ever since. A visible reminder of their meeting is Ricardo's detailed painting of Elba, which hangs over the fireplace. "I was running away from marriage until at age forty-four I met Hanne. She was the woman I had looked for all of my life," he says delightedly.

They visited Italy frequently, and in 1975, captivated by the beauty of the countryside, moved to Tuscany. Eventually they realized that it would always be a comparatively isolated existence for them. "It was beautiful, but a lonely place for us," says Hanne, "like living in a museum focused on classical art."

From Tuscany they went to New York, where Hanne's son was already living. "We visited him there and liked it so much that we came to stay." After being in America for only three weeks Hanne impulsively bought a house in South Hampton, Long Island, but they sold it a year later when Ricardo fell in love with an historic house in East Hampton, which they bought just in time to save from being burned by the local fire department as a training exercise.

"The house, built in 1879, had been vacant for seven years except for a large colony of rodents." Ricardo, who loved doing restoration, spent nine years renovating and planning every detail to preserve its architectural integrity. "Our gift to America," he remarks jokingly. In 1986 they sold the house to violinist Itzhak Perlman, "who still feels he should consult Ricardo before making any changes," says Hanne.

While in East Hampton they both did exceptionally well in the art world, with numerous exhibits. Hanne Brenken's work is in the permanent collections of the Solomon R. Guggenheim Museum and Queens Museum. "Painting for me is like meditation: it comes from the inside. First I let the image emerge, and I let the color flow, then it takes form and I know where I'm going. After coming to America I was compared to Georgia O'Keefe, but while living in Europe I hadn't even seen her work. I was doing fantasy paintings of trees, and people commented that they seemed to represent heads seen from the back with trunks that resembled necks. This prompted me to do a series of forty much more realistic larger-than-life paintings of the backs of heads that I call 'Looking Forward.'" Done in vibrant primary colors, her head collection is a fascinating study in form and composition.

Brenken enjoys painting sculptural plants that to her are "the stuff

Elane Griscom

Ricardo Wiesenberg, named as "one of the eight finest
portrait painters in America," with a detailed
sketch for one of his commissioned portraits.

of dreams." "We had this wild garden in East Hampton with lots of exotic plants," she recalls. "I made them bigger and bigger in my paintings." These powerful works are appropriately titled "Garden of the Giants" and "Land of Silence." Both are part of the series she calls "Meditation Paintings."

Ricardo Wiesenberg's work was also shown widely during their years in East Hampton, and in 1979 he was commissioned to paint the portraits of seven Federal Communications Commissioners in Washington, D.C., as well as other government officials. He first drew detailed sketches of his subjects, working in their offices, and then finished the portraits at home. The work of Hanne and Ricardo was so much in demand in Washington that they sold their East Hampton house, planning to relocate in Washington, D.C., but because of zoning problems

Elane Griscom

Hanne Brenken in the studio with some of her
"Looking Forward" collection.

encountered in building a new studio they finally settled on another historic house in nearby Warrenton, Virginia.

Wiesenberg is a classical realist who does painstakingly detailed sketches of his models before he begins a portrait. Instead of a cold, objective view of his subject, his work is a more personal expression. "When you are a real artist, the hands are the tools of the soul," he comments, and his portraits capture the very essence of his subject. "I love to paint the human figure, and I believe that in the human form are found all the shapes of nature." His classic realism technique has been so successful that he has been named as one of the eight finest portrait artists in America (*Money* magazine, 1990). His landscapes, seascapes, and portraits reflect years of intense academic training.

He goes on to say that his work habits and approach to painting are so different from Hanne's that there is no destructive competition. Also, he has a high energy level at night, and she is an early riser. "I am an optimist and she is a pessimist. Hanne brings the inside world out…. She interprets the world of the subconscious, and I interpret the world of the conscious," he remarks. He paints with much preparation and detailed planning, the technique of a Renaissance master, and she paints intuitively with images "emerging dreamlike" on the canvas.

Despite opposite philosophies and creative techniques, a strong, unifying bond of love and spirituality is always apparent between them.

ℰ Resurrection in the Cemetery

THE SANTA BARBARA Cemetery is situated on one of the most scenic parcels of real estate on the entire South Coast. For a majority of local citizens it is the first choice for a last destination, despite the fact that occasionally some of the cliffside lots erode and slide downhill to the beach. The cemetery scenery, extending over sixty acres, is so spectacular that often tourists in search of the Biltmore Hotel drive into the grounds by mistake. Its beautiful views of mountains, ocean, and Channel Islands are exceptional, even in this area known for its natural beauty.

For European tourists who are knowledgeable about art, the cemetery is number one on their list of places to see in Santa Barbara. Unknown to most locals, the chapel contains the treasured frescoes of world-renowned artist Alfredo Ramos Martinez, and they are rated among the finest mural paintings in the entire country. The general public has taken note of the frescoes only when an occasional controversy arises over attempts to have them scraped off the walls.

The disputed frescoes adorn the walls of a small architectural gem, the chapel designed by George Washington Smith for the cemetery (which was founded in 1867). These major works of art are comparatively unknown. Both Ramos Martinez and architect Smith had studied in Europe, and both were intrigued with Spanish art and architecture. In 1921 Smith began collaborating with the talented draftswoman

Elane Griscom

Dedicated in 1926, the Santa Barbara Cemetery chapel was designed by noted architect George Washinton Smith. The chapel contains the Ramos Martinez frescos, considered to be among the finest works of religious art in the country.

Lutah Maria Riggs on the cemetery chapel design, which was completed in 1926.

The late Donald Bear, founding director of the Santa Barbara Museum of Art, once described the paintings as one of the great achievements of Alfredo Ramos Martinez's impressive career. In 1934, while exhibiting his work throughout California, the Mexican-born Martinez came to Santa Barbara to show his paintings at the Faulkner Gallery. At that time Henry Eichheim, renowned musicologist, and Mary Smith, widow of architect George Washington Smith, commissioned Martinez to create the chapel murals. The Martinez frescoes cost approximately $6,000, and Mrs. Smith and Mr. Eichheim donated them as a gift to the cemetery in memory of Mr. Smith and Mrs. Eichheim.

The late William Bryant, administrative officer of the Santa Barbara Cemetery Association from 1935 to 1980, once commented: "Some members of the cemetery board of directors back in 1935 were unhappy with the murals because they felt they weren't suited to the chapel's classic design. Every time we prepared to scrape them off the walls, word somehow leaked out, and some of the town's leading citizens would intervene."

About the artist Mr. Bryant recalled, "He was a very likable man; I also met his wife and daughter—they were all fine people. It was nothing personal, but I felt the work was too radical and just didn't harmonize with the classic design of the chapel."

Bryant remembered that when he took over as cemetery manager, Alfredo Ramos Martinez was still working on the frescoes. "Scaffolding with iron frames was set up all over the chapel," said Bryant. "I didn't see Martinez for months—he would work on other projects and go back to his Los Angeles studio for long periods of time. It was impossible to sell cremation niches in the chapel and difficult to hold services, so I finally wrote to Martinez and told him that he had a certain number of days left to finish the work, or everything—frescoes and scaffolding—was coming out. Then, of course, Mrs. Smith and Mr. Eichheim also put pressure on Martinez, and the work was finally finished in 1935."

Through the years the Martinez frescoes in the little chapel have been a source of both controversy and inspiration because they are not representative of the usual Judeo-Christian religious art. Martinez, who was a profoundly religious man, transformed the chapel into a symbol of resurrection, utilizing the perfectly proportioned building design to achieve his goal. When the doors to the chapel are open and the murals are illuminated by sunlight, the spectacle is especially breathtaking.

The chapel interior is dominated by a monumental portrait of Christ, hands uplifted in benediction, over the altar. Facing the worshippers seated in the nave, it is centered high above the last arch of the transept in an area topped by a gilt dome. Opposite the Christ portrait, but invisible from the nave, Martinez designed a powerful composition of women, faces buried in their hands, depicting grieving humanity. On the upper half of both sides of the nave walls a procession of monks, nuns, and robed women carry garlands of flowers, coming together above the chapel entrance, where the figure of the risen Christ is surrounded by hosts of angels.

Elane Griscom

*The chapel interior is dominated by the monu-
mental portrait of Christ over the altar
with hands uplifted in benediction.*

The frescoes demonstrate Martinez's genius at filling space in rela-
tion to a given architectural structure. The frescoes are painted in soft,
subtle hues—grays, ochres, browns, and off-whites, with highlights of
blue, green, and warm earth tones.

Martinez excelled at fresco painting, an extremely difficult technique that uses water-based paint applied to wet plaster. It requires the
artist to be a good plasterer as well, because the surface must be
troweled up to a smooth finish, and plaster can only be applied to the
area of wall that will be painted the same day. A full-scale drawing is
done first and then transferred onto the plaster. The water-based paint
penetrates the surface of wet plaster and is then incorporated with it, so
that the paint and plaster dry together. While working on the frescoes,

Elane Griscom

*On both sides of the upper half of the nave walls are a
procession of nuns, monks, and robed women carrying garlands
of flowers. They come together above the chapel entrance, where the
figure of the risen Christ is surrounded by hosts of angels.*

Martinez constantly climbed ladders and scaffolds, sometimes using
brushes with handles five feet long to paint the uppermost areas of the
murals.

Alfredo Ramos Martinez is described as a small, frail man with a
Chaplin-like mustache and unusually large ears. (He blamed the size of
his ears on an irritable childhood math teacher who constantly pulled
them.) His modest appearance contrasted with his importance in the
world of art. Born in Monterrey, Mexico, in 1872, Martinez is known
as the founder of Mexico's modern art movement—an artistic revolu-
tion that coincided with Mexico's political revolutions of this century.

From early childhood Martinez was totally involved with art. At

Elane Griscom

*The Ramos Martinez fresco of the Resurrection is
dramatically placed above the entry to the chapel. The
figure of the resurrected Christ represents eternal life.*

the age of ten he did a portrait of the governor of Monterrey that
earned him a scholarship to the Academia de Bellas Artes in Mexico
City. A nonconformist even then, at the academy he refused to paint
from plaster models used in the classrooms. Instead he painted out of
doors and brought his work to the school only once a year for a
critique.

When he was twenty-two, fortune smiled on him in the guise of a
noted American philanthropist, Phoebe Apperson Hearst, the mother
of William Randolph Hearst. Mrs. Hearst was so impressed with his
talent that she sponsored his art studies, making it possible for him to
study in Paris and in Spain. The French Impressionists made such a
strong impression on him that in later years critics compared him to
Gauguin.

After years spent abroad, Martinez returned home feeling a pro-
found need to establish his Mexican identity. In 1913 he founded the
first of several outdoor schools of painting where students were free from

the traditional classroom situations that he felt destroyed creativity. Martinez's schools paved the way for the well-known Mexican artists of the twentieth century, including his students, David Siqueiros and Jean Charlot.

In 1929 Martinez brought his wife and daughter, Maria, to the United States seeking medical care for Maria, who had been crippled since birth. After unsuccessful treatment at the Mayo Clinic, the family moved to Los Angeles, where Martinez, grieved by his daughter's suffering, began painting religious subjects. Despite being physically frail himself, he was driven by a dynamic spiritual force to create his monumental works. After the cemetery chapel frescoes were finished, he remained in Santa Barbara for another year to create murals for several Montecito homes. Most notable was one of the Madonna painted in an alcove near the entrance to the George Washington Smith residence in Montecito—a gift from Martinez to Mrs. Smith.

In 1946, at the age of seventy-three, Martinez died while in the midst of paining frescoes for the Scripps Memorial Garden in Claremont.

This original elegant chapel building, combined with the pageant of Alfredo Ramos Martinez's magnificent murals, is treasured by the art world and is a fitting memorial to the artistic genius of George Washington Smith and Alfredo Ramos Martinez.